ALADDIN
THE SUPERHERO

Archimedes' Printing Shoppe
& Sundry Goodes

ALADDIN
THE SUPERHERO

ARIN GREENWOOD

ILLUSTRATED BY MICHELE THE PAINTER

Text, photographs and illustrations © 2021
by Aladdin Nation.

All rights reserved. First Edition.

Design by A Little Graphix
Titles and text in Fredricka the Greatest and Chelsea Market
Edited by Lucy Noland and S.J. Russell

No part of this publication may be reproduced, stored in a retrieval system, or transmitted in any form or by any means without prior permission of the publisher.

Library of Congress Cataloging-in-Publication Data

Names: Greenwood, Arin, author. | Gargiulo, Michele Ports, illustrator.
Title: Aladdin the superhero / Arin Greenwood ; illustrated by Michele the Painter.
Description: Philadephia, PA: Archimedes' Printing Shoppe & Sundry Goodes, 2021. | Summary: The inspiring true story of Aladdin, an abused pit-bull type dog, who pays it forward with superhero powers of kindness and compassion after he is saved from certain death.
Identifiers: LCCN: 2021911039 | ISBN: 978-1-955517-02-7
Subjects: LCSH Dogs–Juvenile literature. | Dog rescue–Juvenile literature. | Animal welfare–Juvenile literature. | Pit bull terriers–Juvenile literature. | CYAC Dogs. | Dog rescue. | Animal welfare. | Pit bull terriers. | BISAC PETS / Dogs / General
Classification: LCC HV4746 .G74 2021 | DDC 636.08/32–dc23

Printed on tree-free bamboo paper stock with soy-based eco-friendly inks in China. Cover and spine are 100% recycled Eska®board.

For Hadley and Hanes Kelly,
may you always know the love of a dog.

This book would not be possible without Lilo's Promise Animal Rescue. Jenn, Anita, Heather, Nina and Laura, together we have saved so many lives. Here's to many more. Thank you to my family for always welcoming our fosters and enriching their lives. Finally, to the thousands and thousands of people who love Aladdin from near and far, thank you for always supporting him and for being part of his journey.

Michele Schaffer, Aladdin's Mom

Foreword

Dogs have an incredible power to heal. Just a look, a lick, or a tail wag makes people smile and forget the troubles they have, even if it's just for a moment. Aladdin has that power, but he also has something more. He has resilience and an amazing ability to show love. His mom, Michele, saw this the first time she met him at the shelter. This broken dog who had been through so much was still able to love, even though he was hurting.

Luck blessed both of them that day. Since then, Aladdin and Michele have embarked on a journey where the power of love and kindness conquers all. This is the story of how one extraordinary woman and a super dog found each other and, working together, inspired a nation.

Victoria Stilwell
Dog Behavior Expert and Host of *It's Me or the Dog*

ALADDIN THE SUPERHERO

ALADDIN

THE SUPERHERO

I wish there were a way to make this part of the story easier, but there isn't. So let me tell you from the start that Aladdin, my favorite blocky-headed superhero dog, is okay. Better than okay. He's amazing.

He is MAGIC this dog.

But Aladdin wasn't always okay.

Aladdin hears footsteps and looks up from the floor of his kennel at the animal shelter. The coolness of the concrete makes his hurt body feel better.

Aladdin hasn't been here long—just since the police found him injured by the side of the road. The people at the shelter have been very kind to him, stroking his blocky head, kissing his sweet face and telling him that they are trying to help him.

Aladdin's body hurts. He is so hungry. All of his ribs are sticking out, and he has bald spots because fur does not grow well without nutritious food. But when he hears footsteps, he wags his tail. He feels hope. And love. He just *knows* someone is coming to save him.

That someone is Michele.

She helps a lot of sick dogs. Michele works with a rescue organization called Lilo's Promise. She heard about Aladdin from a kind man at the shelter who knew she would give him good food, love and everything he deserves in the world.

Michele opens the door to Aladdin's kennel. He is so weak, he cannot even stand to greet her, but he wags his tail. Michele gently touches Aladdin's head.

"You will come home with me, and you will always be safe," she promises him.

Aladdin keeps wagging his tail and sighs with relief. He was right to feel hope.

This is where Aladdin's life gets really, really good.

He now lives by the beach in North Wildwood, New Jersey with all the good food he can eat. He's surrounded by new friends and has six new brothers—three dogs and three humans.

Aladdin feels something new: happiness. His body begins to heal. He lifts his nose into the air and sniffs the ocean, food, flowers and friends. He discovers the joy of snacking on potato chips—Pringles in particular. He learns to swim in the ocean and wears a life jacket for when he is too tired to paddle.

Aladdin's fur grows back, thick and caramel colored, nearly the same color as Michele's hair. This sameness does not mean much to Aladdin, but to Michele it is a special connection.

Every day is better than the day before.

Aladdin rests his head in the crook of Michele's arm as he dozes and snores. Even while he sleeps, his tail wags.

Michele is very happy too. Sometimes she sits by the ocean and stares at Aladdin while listening to the waves. She kisses his head over and over. "I love you Aladdin," Michele whispers in his floppy, fuzzy ears. Aladdin licks her cheek and leans his body closer to hers.

Michele was going to foster Aladdin until he was well then find him a wonderful home with a family of his own. This is how Michele and Lilo's Promise usually help dogs, by getting them through the hard times then sending them off to be happy and loved.

This time though, Michele realizes Aladdin has a family.

He is already home. Her home is his home. And she and Aladdin will live together in this house by the sea, snack on potato chips, take long naps, swim in the ocean and love each other their whole lives.

Aladdin now feels better, so Michele introduces him to more people. Aladdin is shy at first. Michele understands why. Not all of his experiences with people have been good. Little by little, he gains confidence and makes more friends.

Before long, Aladdin has many friends. He has the ballerina who lives next door and her granddaughter Willow.

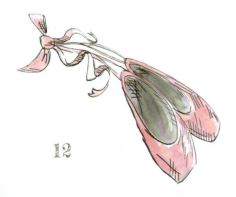

He's friends with a professional football player for the Baltimore Ravens who visits Aladdin at the beach.

He has his human brothers' friends and Michele's friends. And soon every person that he encounters becomes a friend.

Aladdin loves people.

And people love him right back.

Whenever Aladdin is with a friend, old or new, Michele notices he seems to glow from within.

More than that, Aladdin just knows who really needs him. If someone is feeling scared, sad or alone, Aladdin walks right up to them. He sits by them, leans in closely and gives them doggie kisses. His tail wags and wags. Soon they start to smile.

Everyone tells Michele that no matter how they are feeling, when they meet Aladdin, they feel better. There is something about his sweet face, his wagging tail and his lovingness that works like medicine . . . or magic.

I can tell you from experience this is true.

Michele has a great idea.

"Would you like to become a therapy dog?" Michele asks Aladdin. Aladdin wags his tail while snacking on another potato chip. Michele takes this as an enthusiastic "yes!"

Therapy dogs go to hospitals and schools and other places where people sometimes could really use a friend. They will sit with you while you whisper your problems in their ears. Or if you just want to sit quietly, that's fine too.

You can hug a therapy dog and rub the dog's belly. The pup just wants you to feel better.

Michele takes Aladdin to therapy dog school. He does great! He learns to sit and stay, and really listen hard when someone is talking to him. Aladdin feels compassion and empathy.

Aladdin and Michele study hard and pass the therapy dog test with flying colors. Aladdin gets a special certificate that lets him visit hospitals, schools and wherever else he is needed.

Aladdin's friend makes him a bright green superhero costume so people can see right away how special he is. Aladdin wears it proudly.

Michele brings Aladdin to a hospital for his first visit. She feels nervous. What if he doesn't know what to do? What if he gets scared?

But he's not scared. Aladdin knows exactly what to do.

The first person he meets is ME.

I am lying in a bed in a hospital room under several blankets because I am so cold. I'm always cold. My mom is with me. She reads while I watch cartoons and holds my hands to warm me.

I hear footsteps and look up. Is that a dog in the doorway, wearing a green mask and a cape like a superhero?! I smile for the first time in what feels like forever.

The nice woman holding the dog's leash introduces herself as Michele. "And this is Aladdin," she says pointing at the dog in the green costume.

Aladdin doesn't know it–couldn't know it–but just at that moment, I had been missing my dog Bella so much.

It's hard being in the hospital. It's hard being away from Bella.

I look at my mom. "Can I?" I ask. And she nods.

I pat my bed. "Come here," I say to the dog. "If you want to, I mean."

Michele lets Aladdin off his leash, and he runs to me and leaps up onto my bed. He snuggles up and wags his tail. It goes thump, thump, thump against my leg.

"Tell him anything you want," Michele says. "And hug him too, if you'd like."

I hug Aladdin and whisper in his ear for a long, long time. I tell him everything I am feeling, everything I am afraid of, everything that hurts. I tell him that my hair is usually golden colored, but it's all gone now because of my treatments. And even though my mom kisses my head and tells me it will all grow back, I am not sure she is right, and I'm scared.

I tell him that I miss my brother and sister, and my dog Bella, who has a brown coat, a short tail and a smushed nose. Bella is my best friend in the world. I tell him that I hope Bella hasn't forgotten me, and I hope that she is getting enough treats and walks while I am here trying to get better.

Aladdin leans into me. He licks my arm, right at the spot where I had a needle. My arm feels better. I hug Aladdin and I sigh, feeling something that I have not felt in a very long time:

HAPPINESS.

I am the first person that Aladdin meets as a therapy dog, but I am far from the last. Within a short time, he becomes one of the most famous therapy dogs that ever lived. Aladdin visits thousands of people from across the country. He goes from coast to coast and all in between.

Everywhere he goes people grow happier than they were before they met him.

I am telling you he's MAGICAL.

Aladdin and Michele start teaching classes at schools, offices and other busy places. They teach how love and kindness can make things better, how love and kindness can change the world.

With the help of many professional football players, Aladdin has spread the importance of love and kindness far and wide.

Aladdin is so amazing, he gets invited to appear on television to help even more people. It's incredible seeing my friend on TV being treated like the star he is.

Aladdin wears his green costume while a famous talk show host in a fancy suit pets him, sings to him and loves on him. People everywhere get to experience his joy and see a dog who overcame everything and now gives everything through love.

I leave the hospital soon after Aladdin makes his first television appearance. He will be on TV many more times in the years to come.

I am finally well and get to go home and be with my family and Bella again. Bella remembers me! I give her lots of treats and we go on lots of walks. I'll never forget the feeling of Aladdin's tail thumping against my leg or the feeling of his soft ear against my lips while I whispered to him.

I stay in touch with Aladdin, and I visit him at his house by the beach. Mom drives me there. She smiles all the time now. Aladdin and I swim in the ocean together, eat potato chips and hang out with Willow, the ballerina's granddaughter.

Even though he is famous and I am no longer sick, Aladdin lets me hug him and share my secrets and fears, and all the things that I am excited about too. He does not always wear his green superhero costume when we hang out. I know he is special even without his suit.

On one of our visits, Michele tells me about Aladdin's sad past and his happy rescue.

Michele believes Aladdin is so kind and so good because he has also suffered and understands what it is to need love.

Perhaps he remembers the kindness he was shown when he was so hurt, and he wants to repay it.

Or perhaps this is just Aladdin. He is good and he is kind. He loves and he is loved.

Michele is so proud of him and so grateful for this

magical dog.

And so am I.

SUPERHEROES

Photo by Valerie Bruder

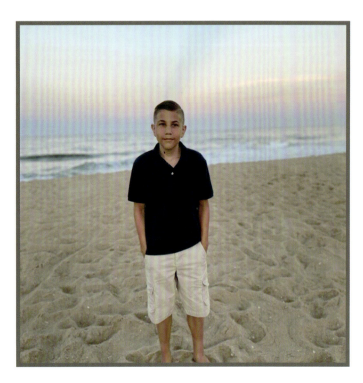

2013 is the year each changed the other's life. In the years since Michele Schaffer laid eyes on the pup she would name Aladdin, he has become a Ronald McDonald House Ambassador, helping children like Ryan. Named the American Humane Therapy Dog of the Year in 2017, Aladdin has appeared on television shows from *Harry* with Harry Connick Jr. to *TODAY*. Though Laddy, as he is affectionately known, has a more impressive résumé than most humans, his favorite thing is to sit in someone's lap, and love and be loved.

Ryan Arevalo beat medulloblastoma at the tender age of 13. Doctors say he is now cancer-free. Ryan loves social studies and football, especially the Baltimore Ravens—Michele and Aladdin helped him meet the team! One day, he wants to be a CEO. Aladdin will always have a special place in Ryan's heart: "Meeting Aladdin at the Ronald McDonald House was my favorite part of staying there. He always gave me something to look forward to."

AUTHOR AND ILLUSTRATOR

Arin Greenwood is an animal welfare writer, former lawyer, and novelist living in St. Petersburg, Florida. She was *The Huffington Post*'s animal welfare editor, and her stories about cats, dogs, and other critters have been published in *The Dodo*, *The Washington Post*, *Slate*, *TODAY*'s website, the *American Bar Association Journal*, and other publications. Arin is author of *Your Robot Dog Will Die*, published by Soho Teen in 2018. She wants to pet your dog.

Michele Ports Gargiulo (Michele the Painter) has melded her two great loves, art and animals, for the greater good. For every single sale she makes, she donates to an animal rescue. Since 2014, she's donated more than $30,000 in art and funds. When Aladdin trotted into her life, Michele fell in love and immediately started painting him. She even designed an Aladdin T-shirt. She is thrilled that her art graces the pages of *Aladdin the Superhero*–Michele's favorite pup, right after her beloved S'mores.

WWW.FACEBOOK.COM/ALADDINNATION